A New Tune A Day™
Performance Pieces *for* Violin

Compiled and arranged by Ned Bennett

Chord symbols for all pieces are included for guitar or keyboard accompaniment.

Boston Music Company

Contents

Published by
Boston Music Company
Exclusive Distributors:
Contact us:
Hal Leonard
7777 West Bluemound Road
Milwaukee, WI 53213
Email: info@halleonard.com

In Europe, contact:
Hal Leonard Europe Limited
42 Wigmore Street
Marylebone, London, W1U 2RN
Email: info@halleonardeurope.com

In Australia, contact:
Hal Leonard Australia Pty. Ltd.
4 Lentara Court
Cheltenham, Victoria, 3192 Australia
Email: info@halleonard.com.au

Compiled and edited by Ned Bennett
Series Editor: David Harrison
Music processed by Paul Ewers Music Design
Cover and book designed by Chloë Alexander
Photography by Matthew Ward
Printed in the US
Backing tracks by Guy Dagul
CD recorded, mixed and mastered by
Jonas Persson and John Rose

Camptown Races

Foster

Moderately

C G C

mf

G C F

f

C Dm/F G7 C

Early One Morning

Traditional

3

Moderately

G C D

mf

G C D7 G

D7 G D7 G

C Am D7sus D7 G

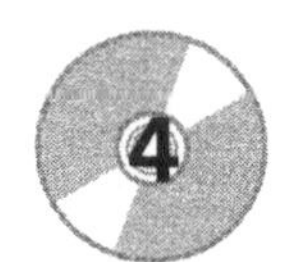

Santa Lucia

Neapolitan Traditional

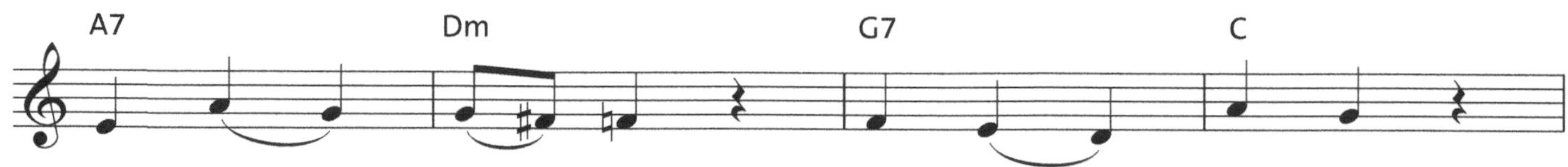

Poor Little Buttercup (from *HMS Pinafore*)

Sullivan

Gently

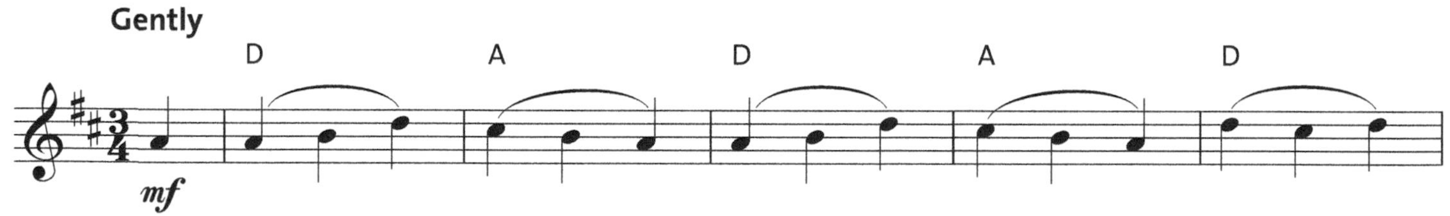

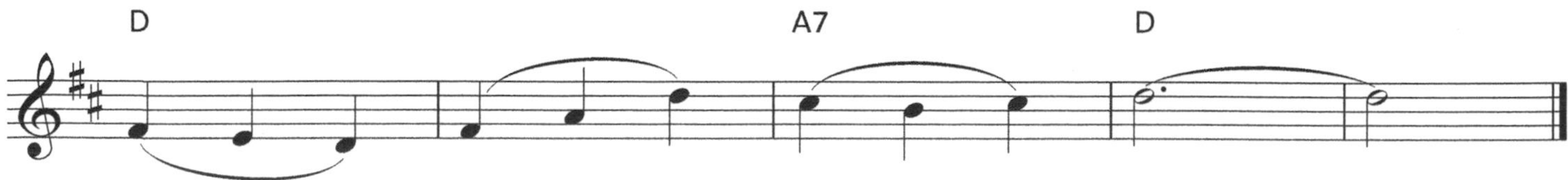

My Bonnie Lies Over The Ocean

Scottish Traditional

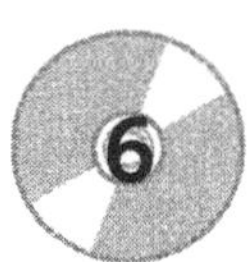

Smoothly

Romance No. 1

Beethoven

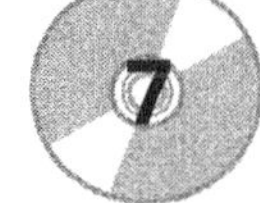

Smoothly

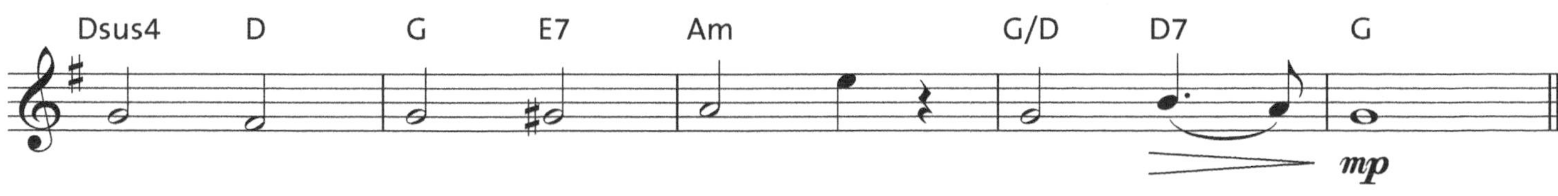

Kalinka

Russian Traditional

Moderato

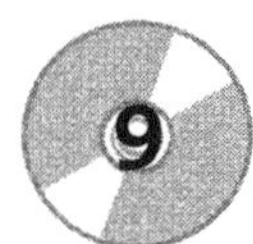

Coventry Carol

16th Century English

Gently

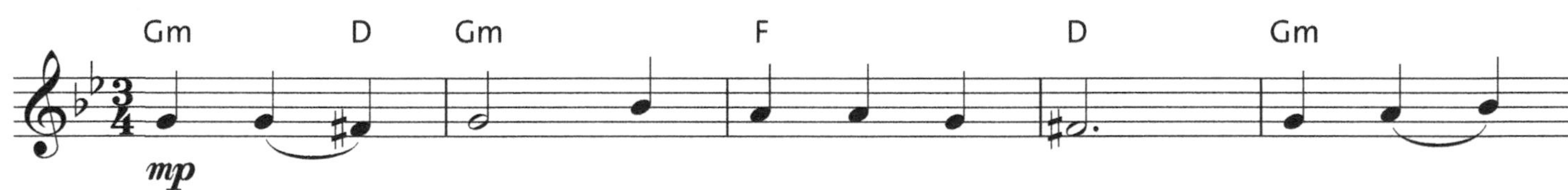

Molly Malone

Yorkston

Gently

Banana Boat Song

Jamaican Traditional

11

Moderately

Telstar

Meek

Moderately quick

C Am Dm7 G7 C Am7

f

F G7 C/E Am F G

1. 2.

C Am Dm G7 Dm G7

C Am Dm 3 G7 C Am

mf

Dm 3 G7 C Am Dm 3 G7

C Am Dm 3 G7 3

C Am Dm7 G7 C Am7

f

F G7 C/E Am F G C

Am Dm G7 C F C

Satin Doll

Ellington, Strayhorn & Mercer

Moderate swing

Am7 D7 Am7 D7 Bm7 E7 Bm7 E7

mp

Am7 E♭m7 A♭7 G E7

Am7 D7 Am7 D7 Bm7 E7 Bm7 E7

mf

Am7 Ebm7 A♭7 G

f

Dm7 G7 Dm7 G7 C

Em7 A7 Em7 A7 Am7 D7

Am7 D7 Am7 D7 Bm7 E7 Bm7 E7

mf

Am7 E♭m7 A♭7 G Am7 A♭7 G

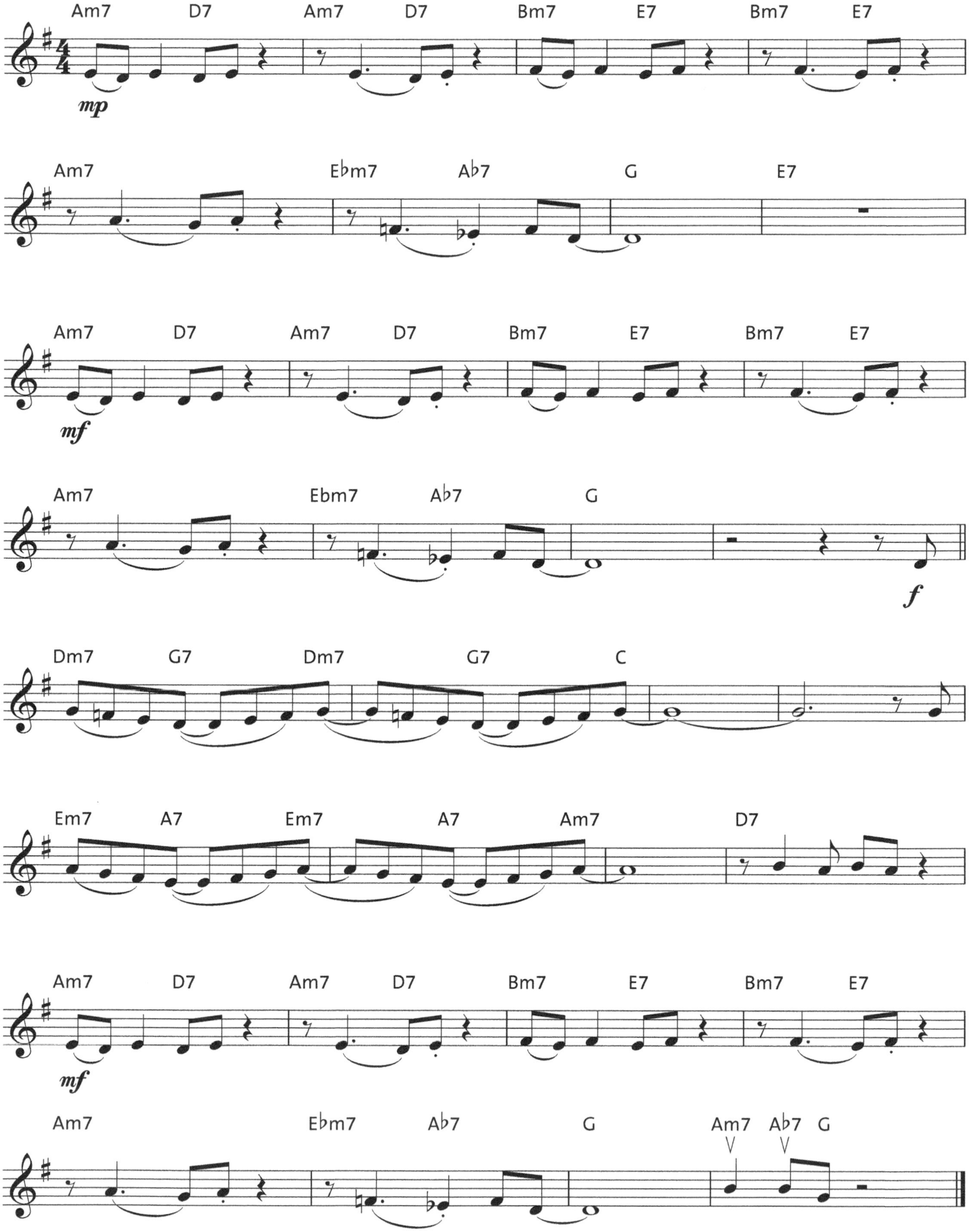

14 *Coasts Of High Barbary*

American Traditional

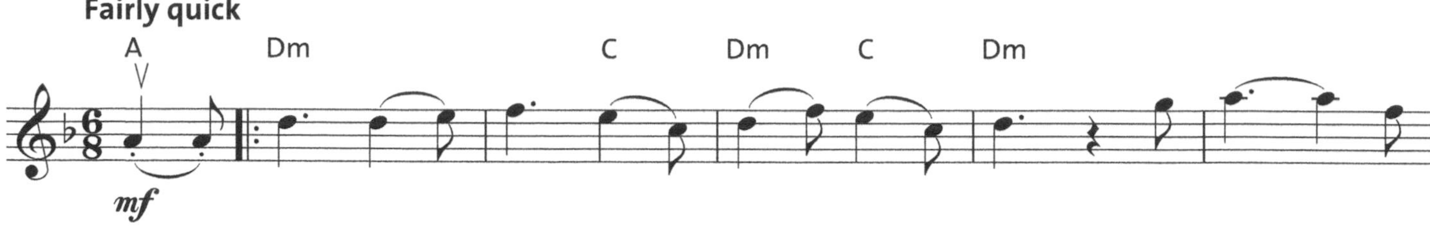

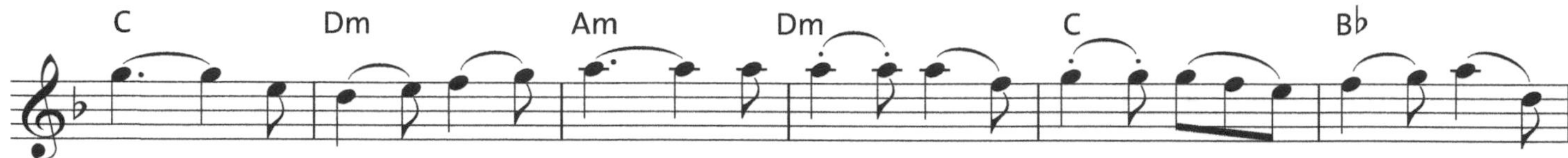

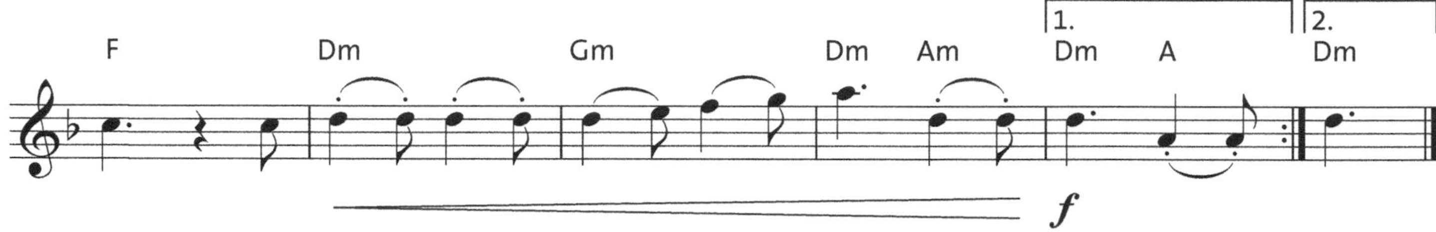

Babu Sau

Ngizim Traditional

Mama Don't Allow

American Traditional

16

Lively swing
G
f
D7
G
G7
C
Cdim7
G
E7
A7
D7
G

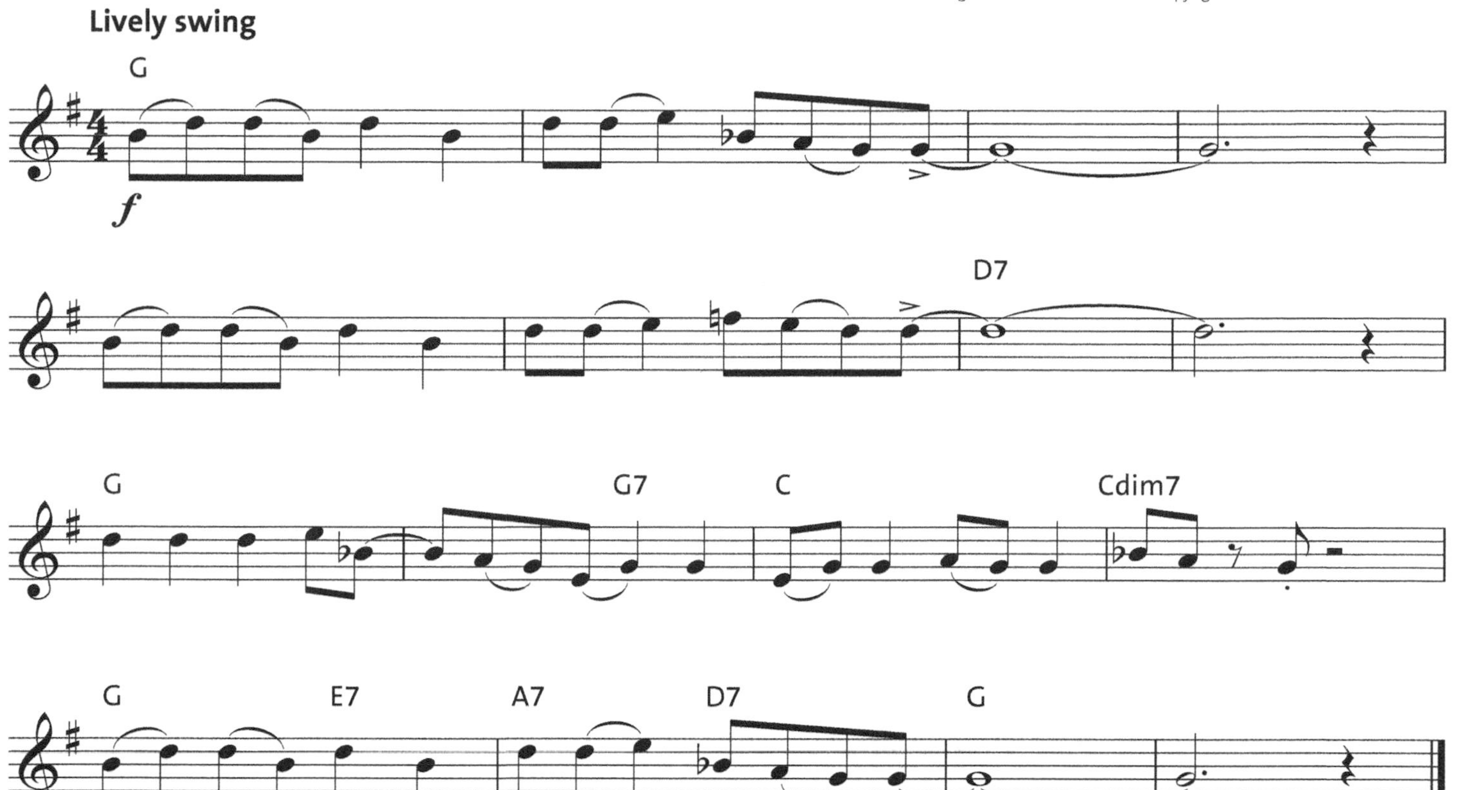

La Cucaracha

Mexican Traditional

17

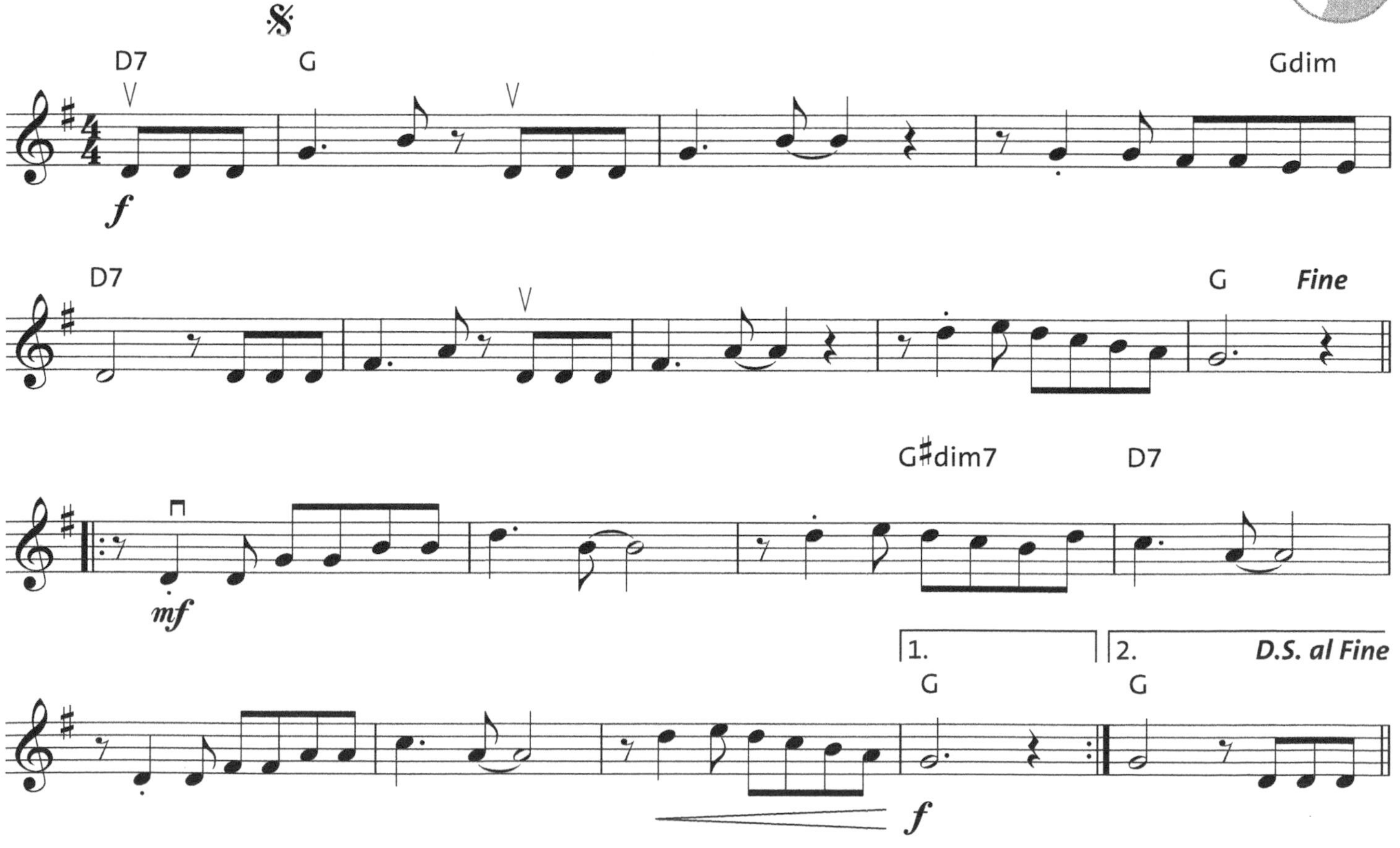
D7
G
Gdim
f
D7
G
Fine
G♯dim7
D7
mf
1.
2.
D.S. al Fine
G
G
f

18 *Shenandoah*

American Traditional

Gently

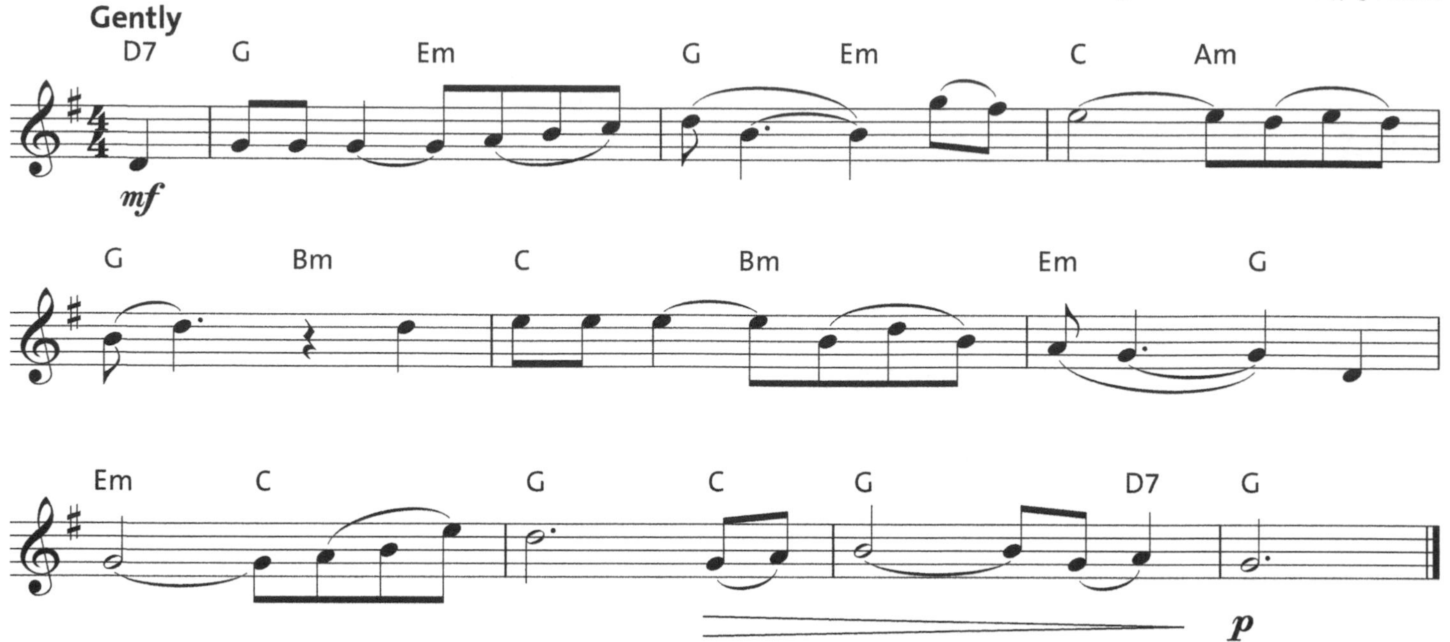

19 *Turkey In The Straw*

American Traditional

Moderately quick

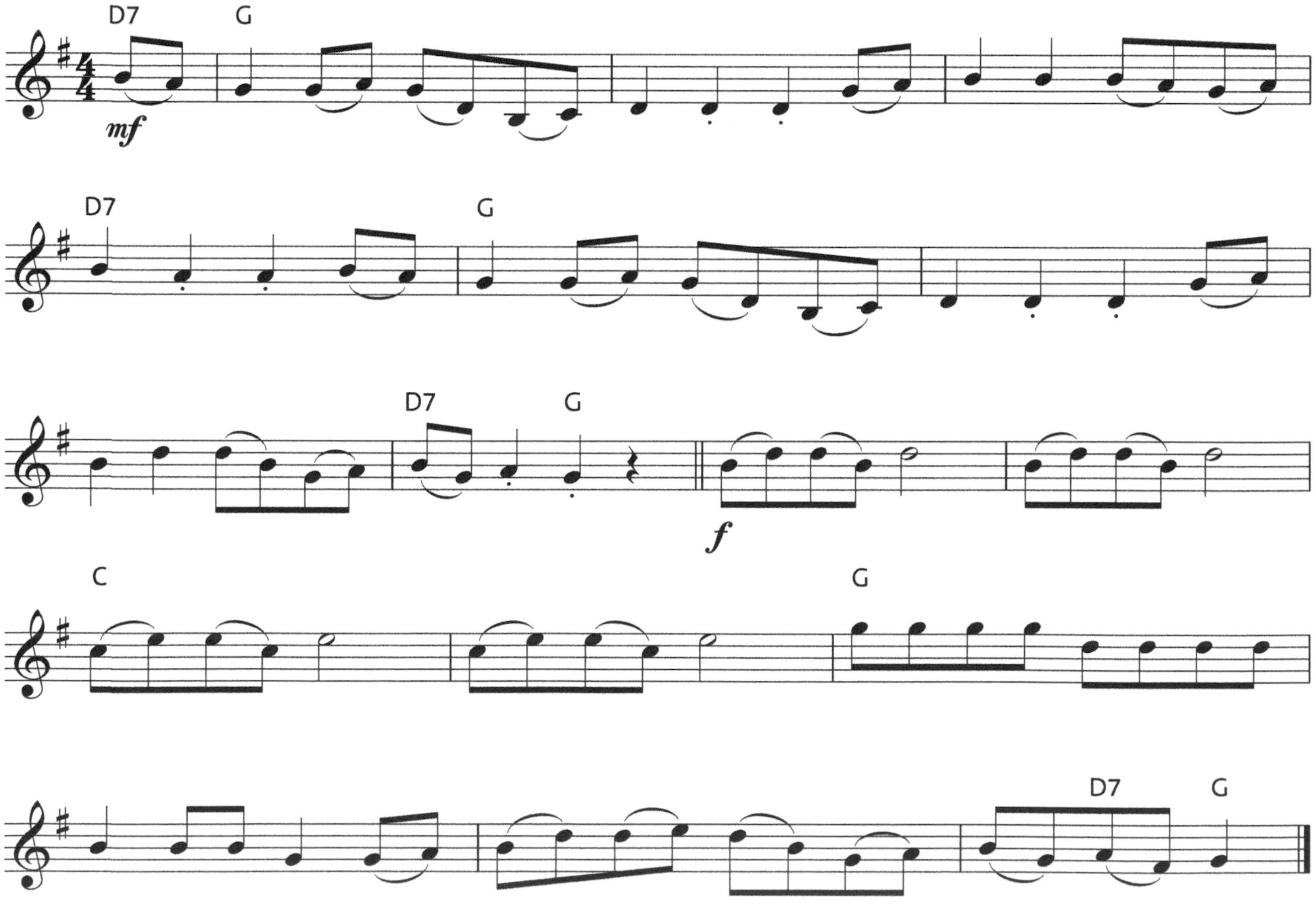

Steal Away

Spiritual

20

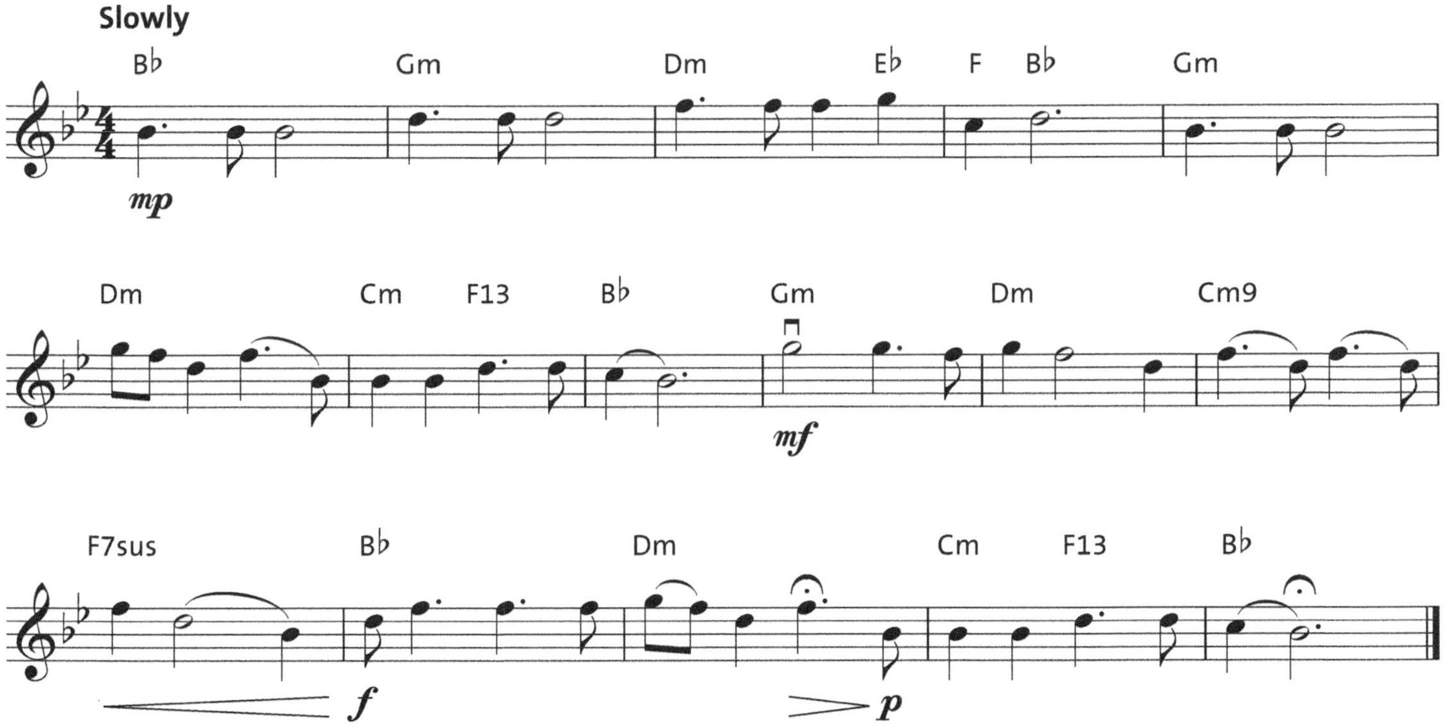
Slowly
B♭
Gm
Dm
E♭
F
B♭
Gm
mp
Dm
Cm
F13
B♭
Gm
Dm
Cm9
mf
F7sus
B♭
Dm
Cm
F13
B♭
f
p

Over The Hills

British Traditional

21

Moderately
A
D
G
D
mp
A
D
G
G/A
D
A
D
G
D
mf
A
D
G
D

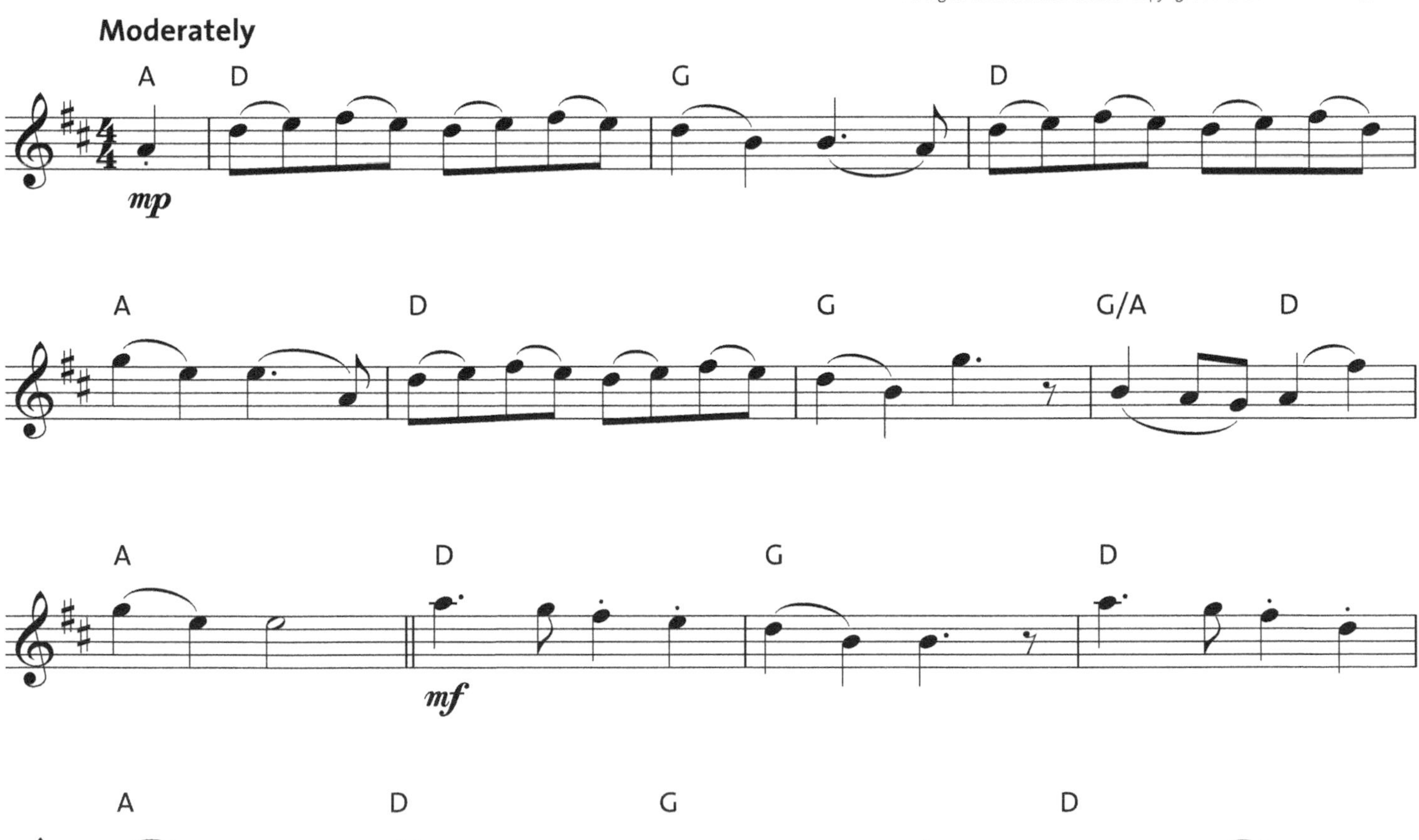

Catch A Falling Star

Vance & Pockriss

Underneath The Arches

McCarthy, Flannigan & Connely

Slow swing

G7 C Am7 D7
mp

G7 C

Aaug A7 D7
mf

G7

C Am7 D7
mp

Dm7 G7 B7 E7
mf

A7 Aaug A7 D7

Dm7 G7 C Fm C

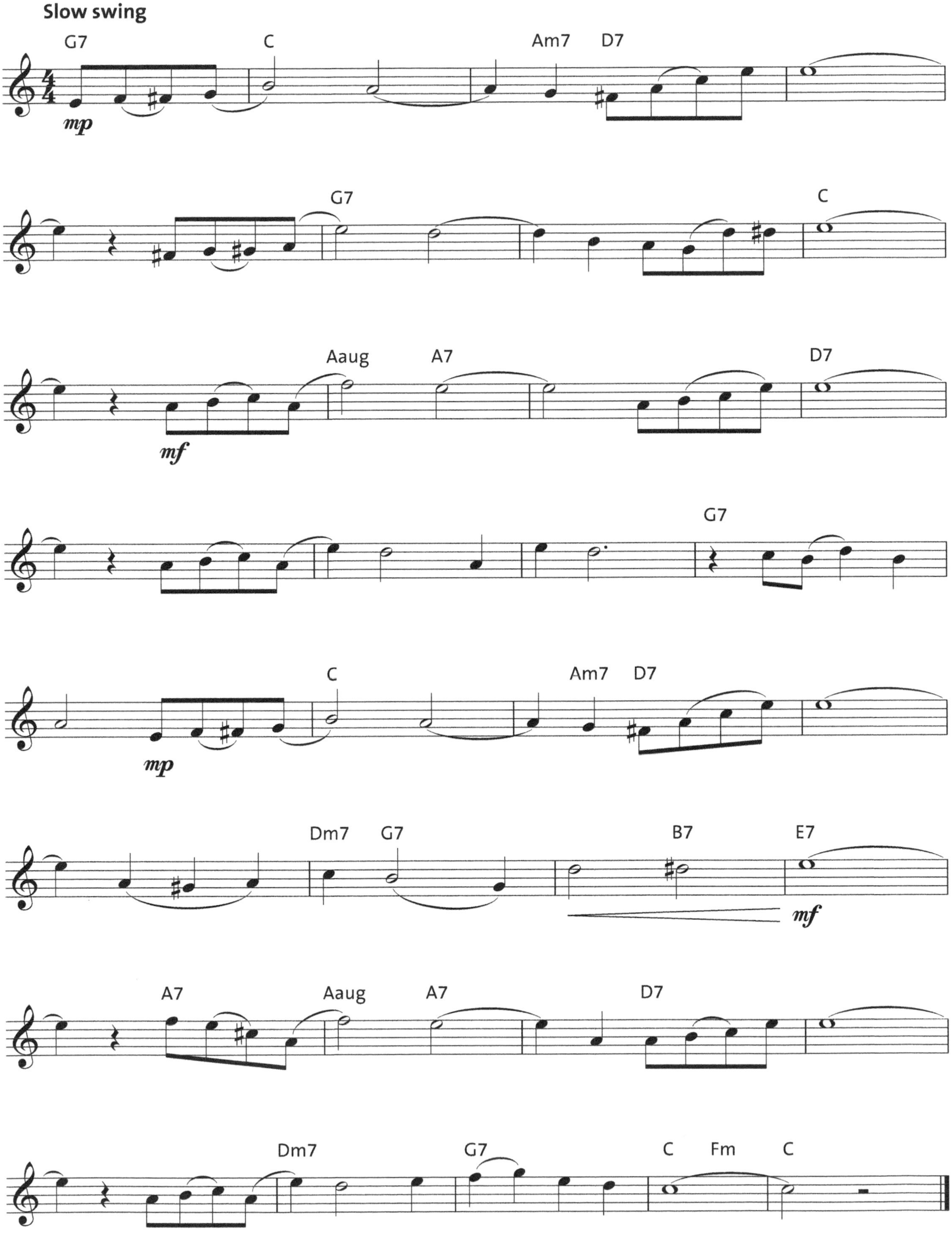

24 Ding Dong Merrily On High

16th Century French

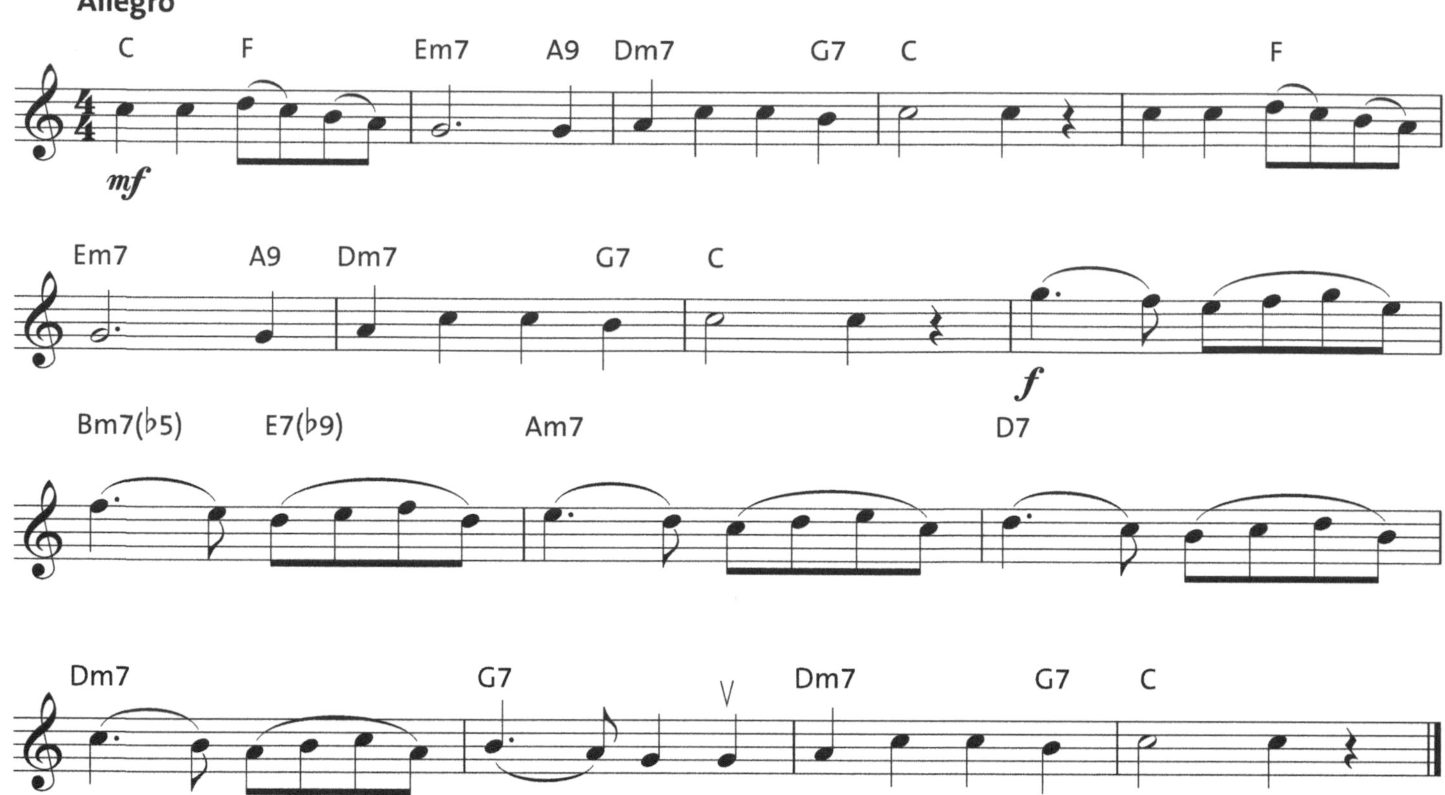

By The Rivers Of Babylon

Caribbean Traditional

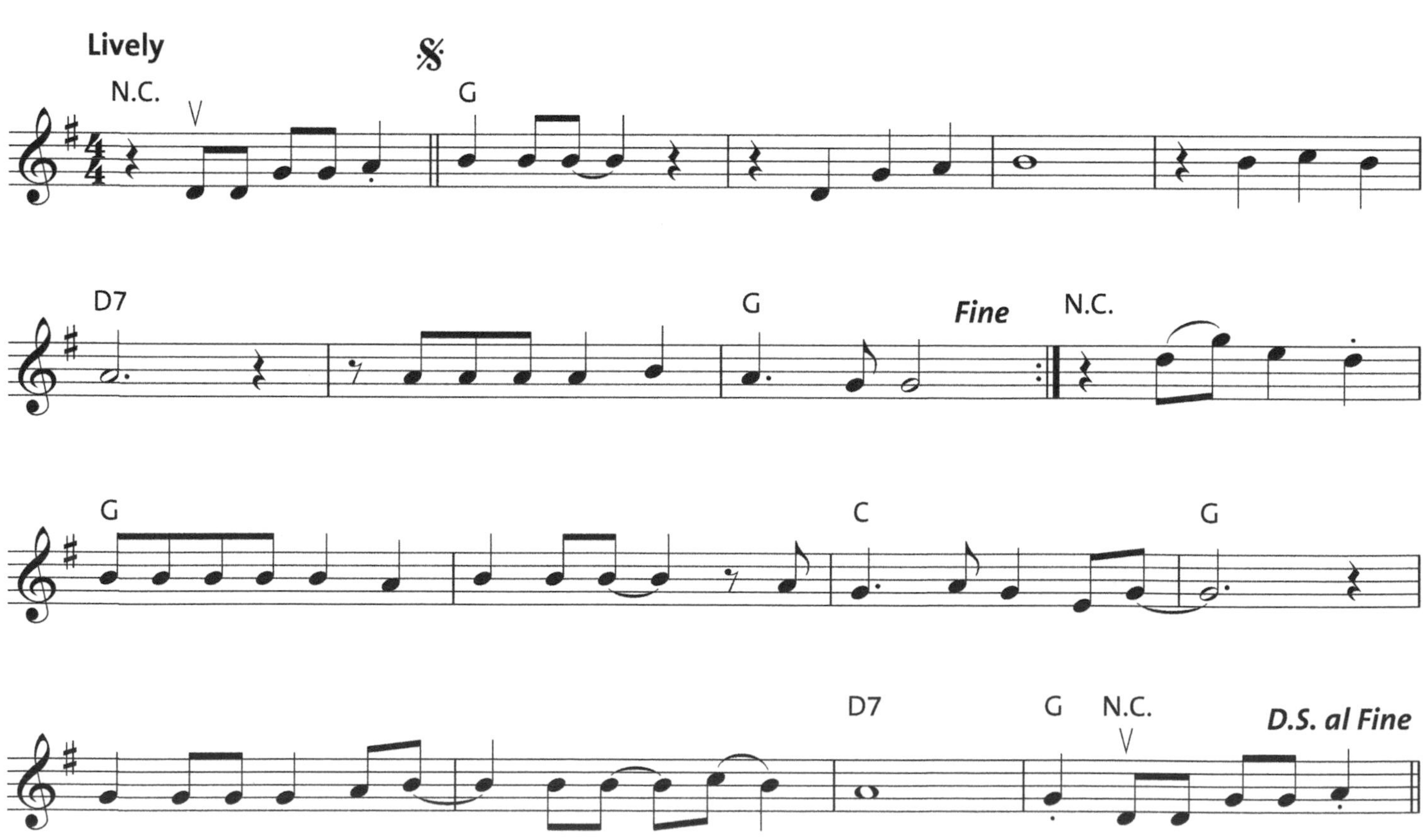

Old Folks At Home

Foster

Minuet

Bach

Poco allegro

G C G Am D7

f

G 1. D G D 2. Am/C D G

D Em A

mp

D A7 D7 G C G

mf

D G D G

f

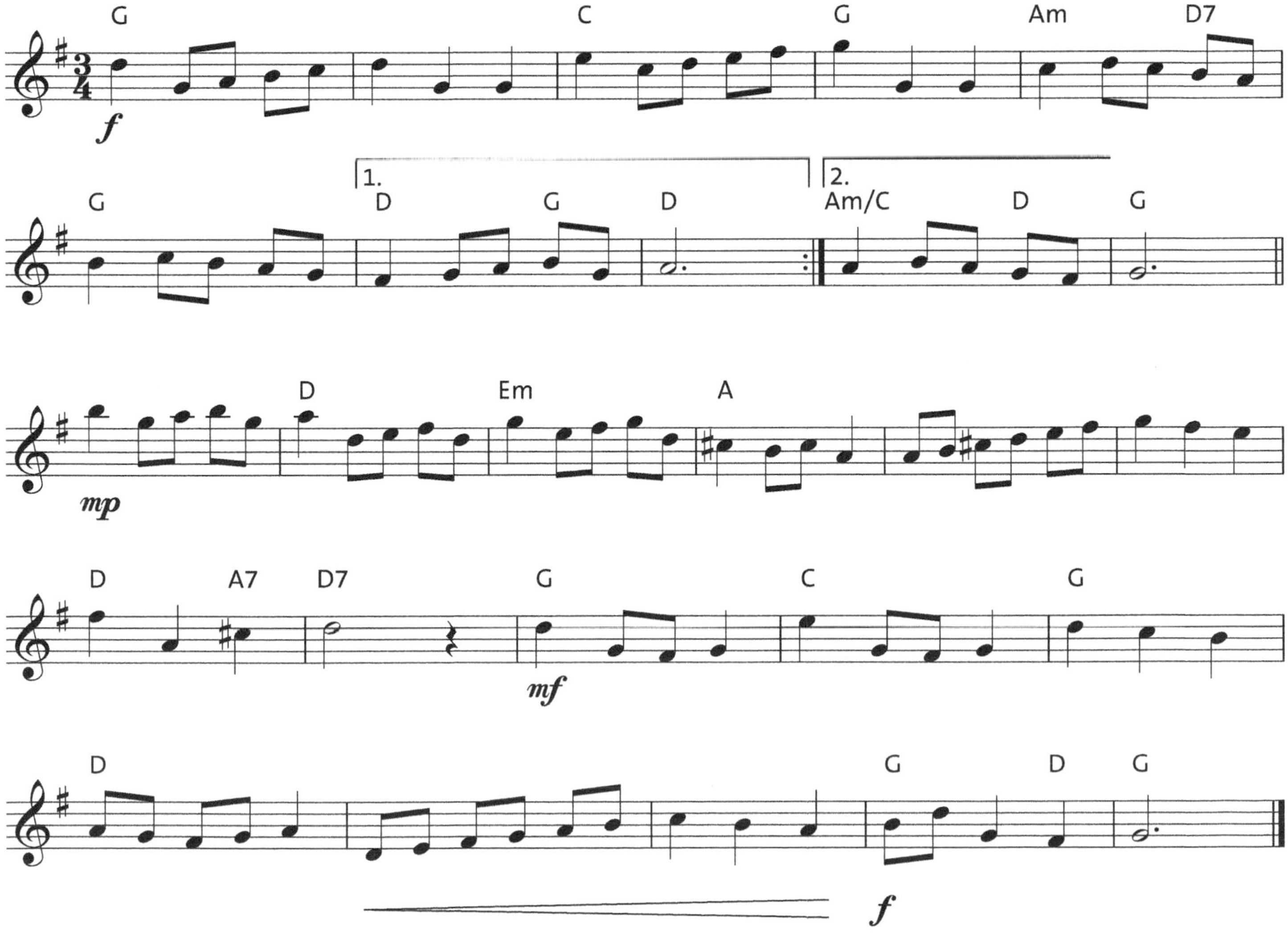

28 Jurassic Park Theme

Williams

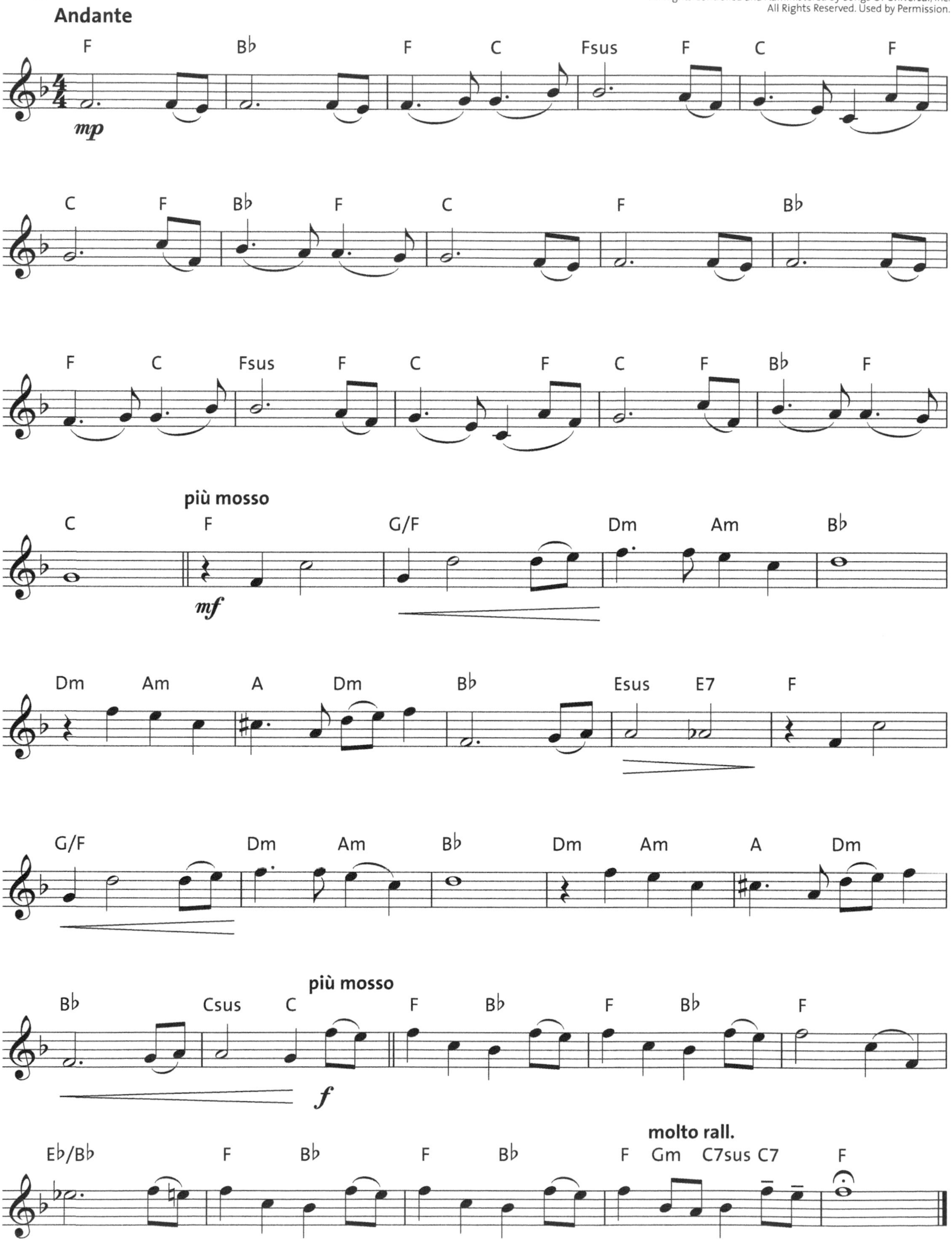
Andante
F Bb F C Fsus F C F
mp
C F Bb F C F Bb
F C Fsus F C F C F Bb F
più mosso
C F G/F Dm Am Bb
mf
Dm Am A Dm Bb Esus E7 F
G/F Dm Am Bb Dm Am A Dm
più mosso
Bb Csus C F Bb F Bb F
f
molto rall.
Eb/Bb F Bb F Bb F Gm C7sus C7 F

Angel Eyes

Brent & Dennis

29

30 *Dick's Maggot*

Scottish Traditional

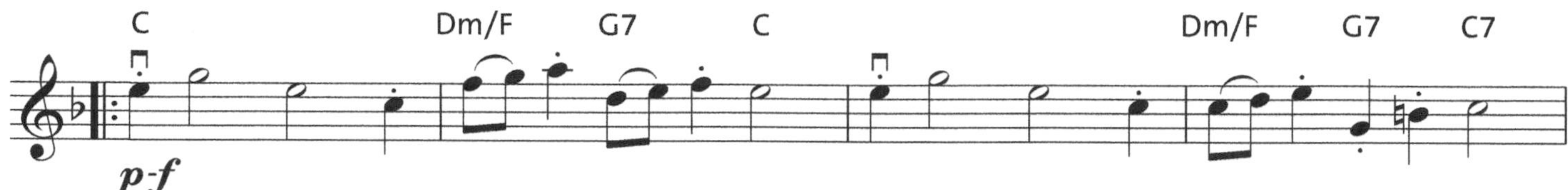

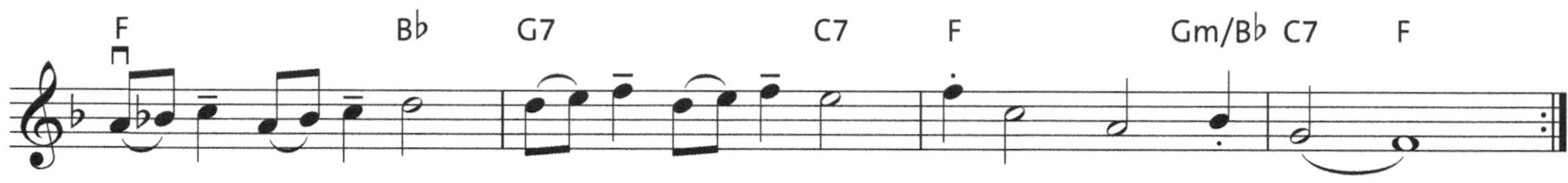

Nobody Knows

Burleigh

British Grenadiers

British Traditional

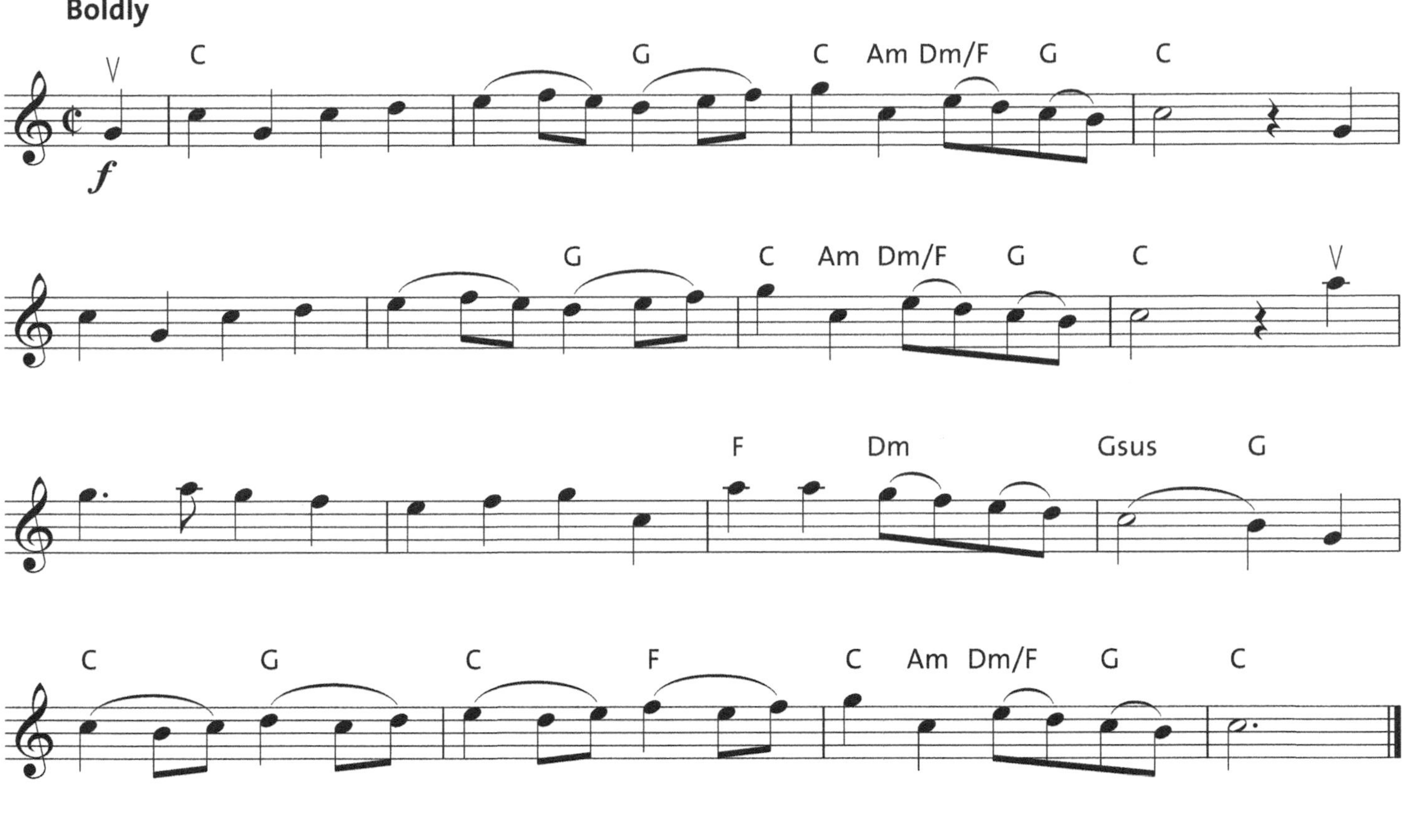

Minuet

Mozart

34 *Greensleeves*

English Traditional

Flowing

35 *The Hebrides Overture* (excerpt)

Mendelssohn

Andante espressivo

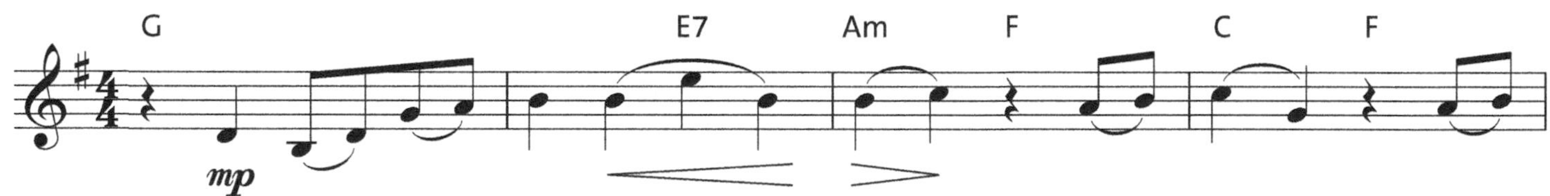

The Keel Row

Scottish Traditional

36

Mexican Hat Dance

Mexican Traditional

37

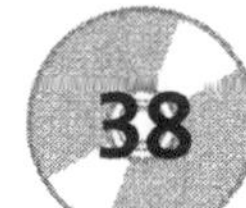

38 *Perdido*

Tizol

Swing

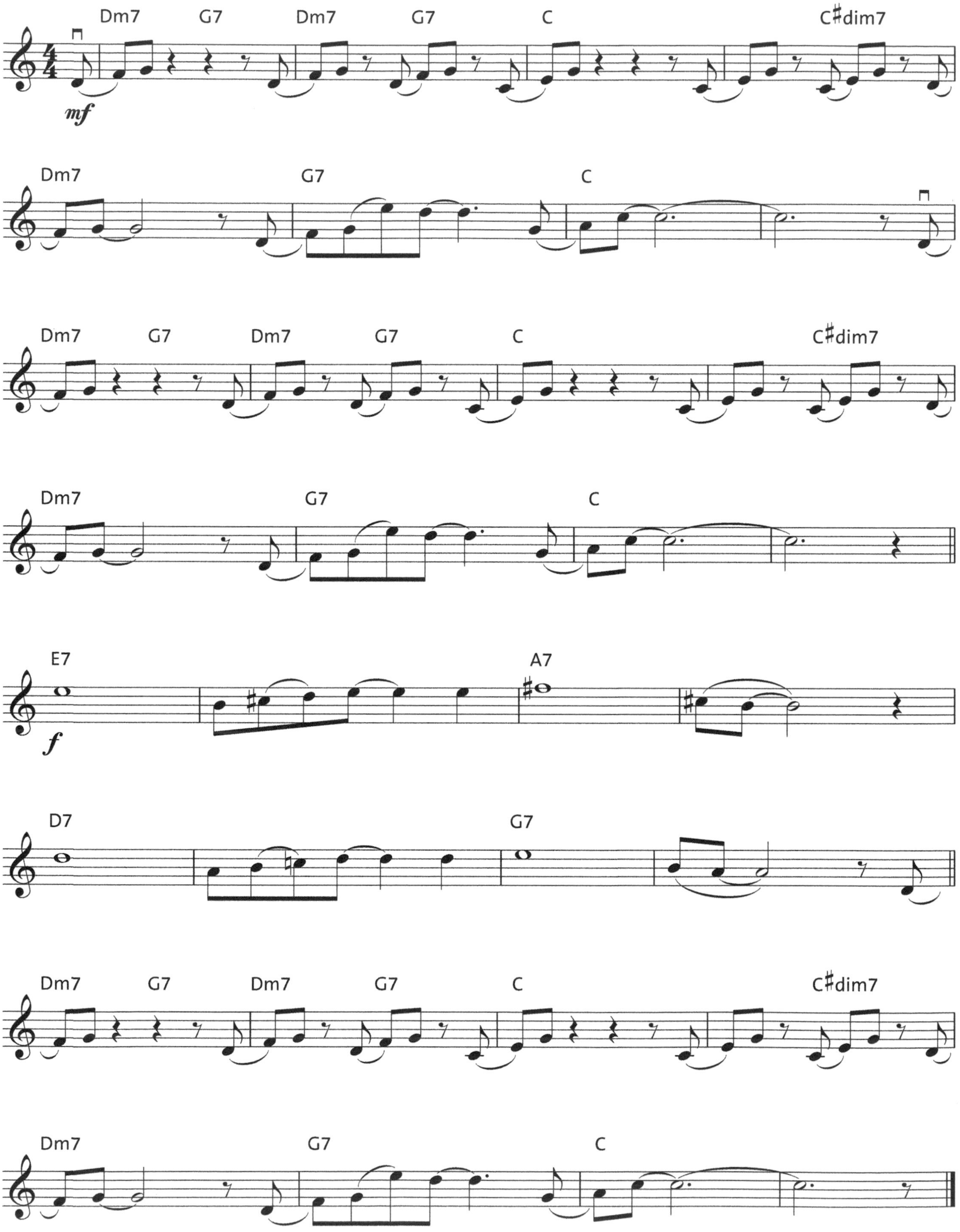
Dm7 G7 Dm7 G7 C C♯dim7
mf
Dm7 G7 C
Dm7 G7 Dm7 G7 C C♯dim7
Dm7 G7 C
E7 A7
f
D7 G7
Dm7 G7 Dm7 G7 C C♯dim7
Dm7 G7 C

Blackadder Theme

Goodall

39

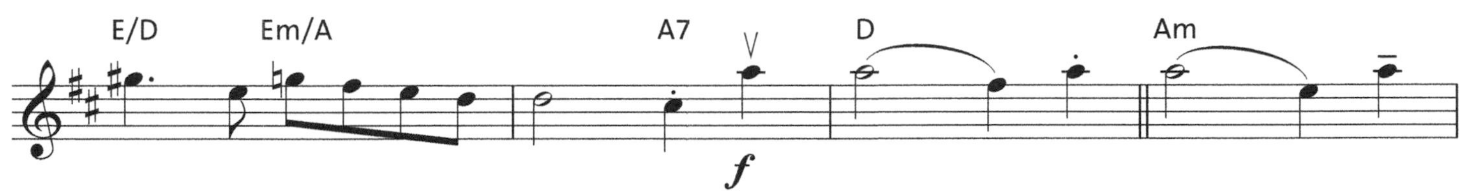

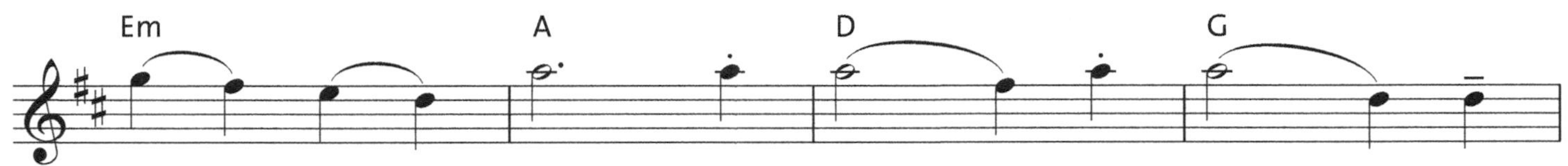

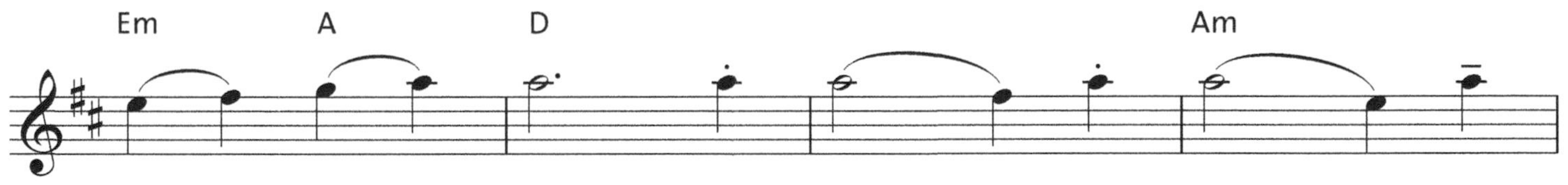

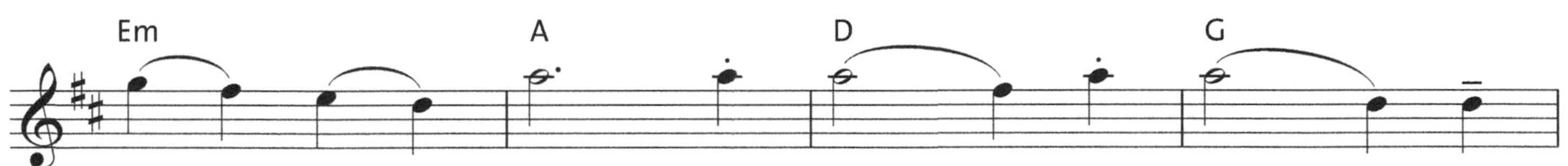

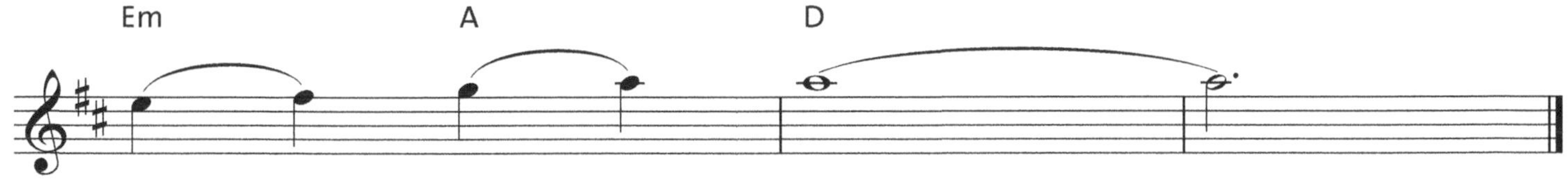

Deep River

Spiritual

Calmly

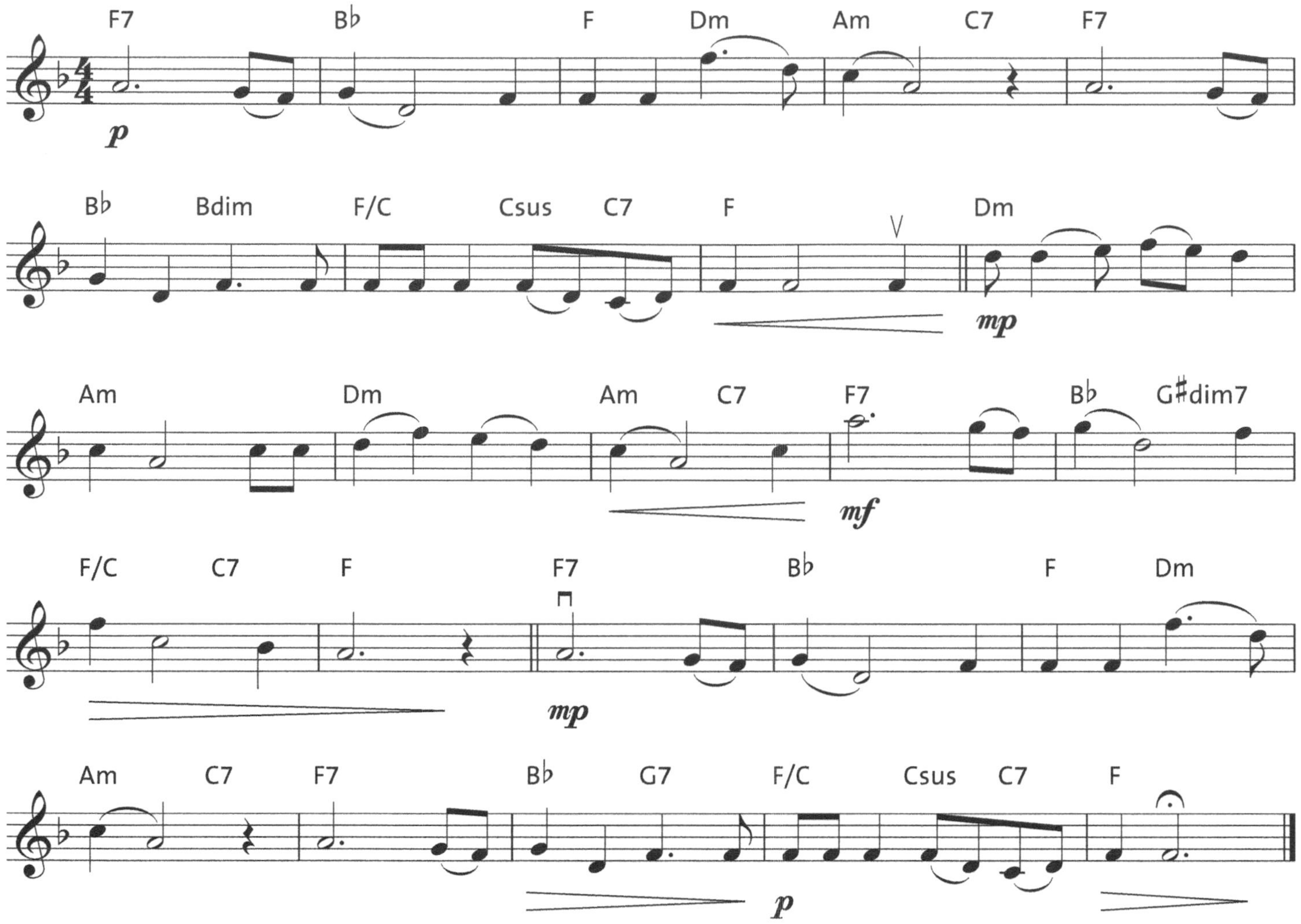

F7 B♭ F Dm Am C7 F7

p

B♭ Bdim F/C Csus C7 F Dm

mp

Am Dm Am C7 F7 B♭ G♯dim7

mf

F/C C7 F F7 B♭ F Dm

mp

Am C7 F7 B♭ G7 F/C Csus C7 F

p

Das Wandern

Zöllner

Hatikvah

Cohen

The Ash Grove

Welsh Traditional

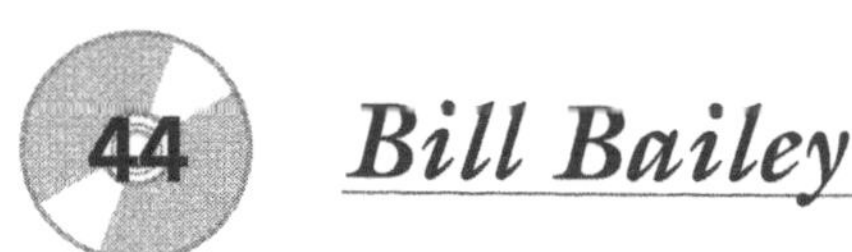

44 *Bill Bailey*

American Traditional

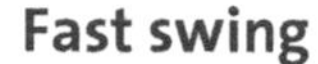

Fast swing

A
f
E7
A
A7
D7
D♯dim7
A/E
F♯7
B7
E7
A

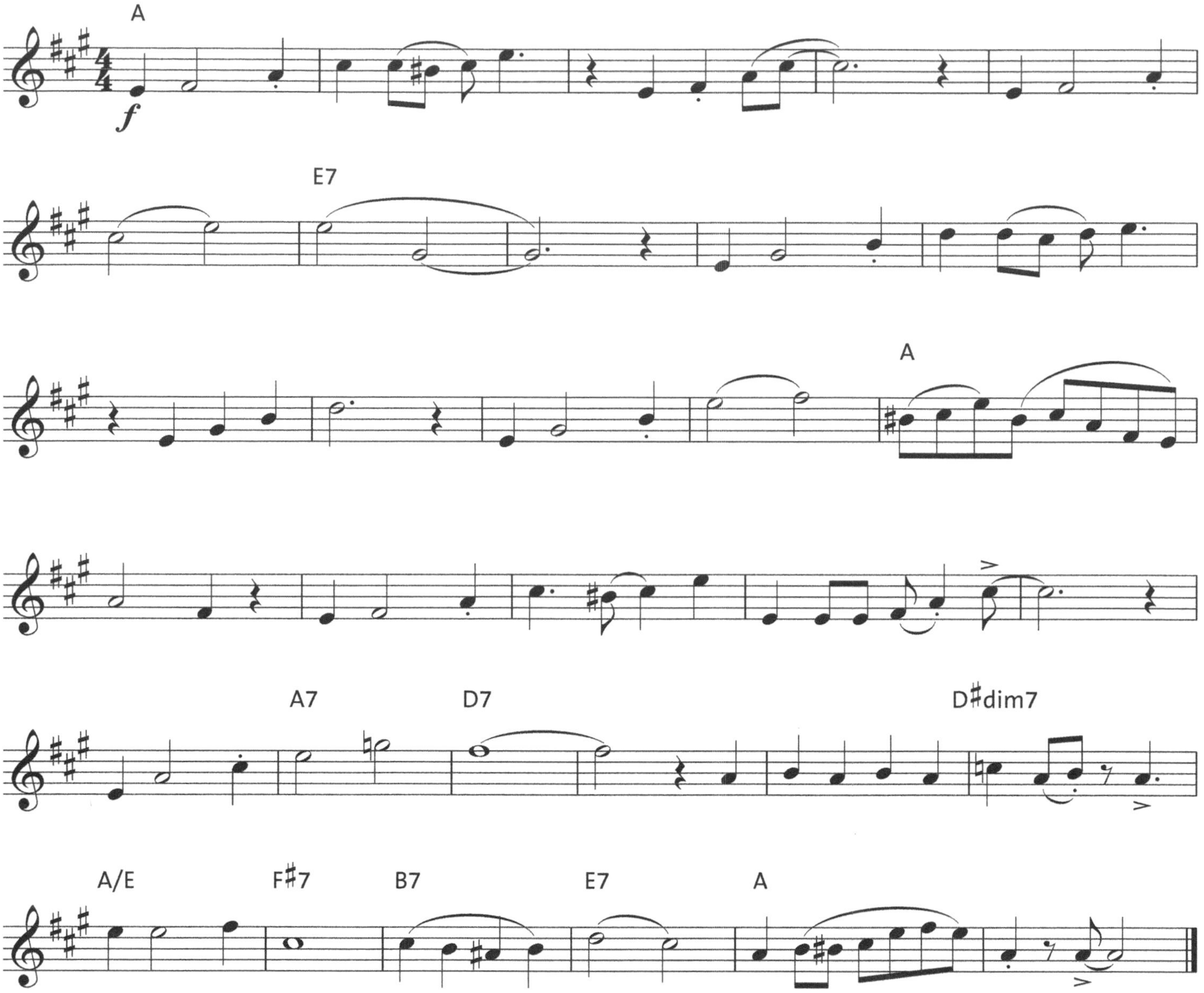

45 *Tit Willow* (from *The Mikado*)

Sullivan

Moderato

F
B♭
F
mf
C
F

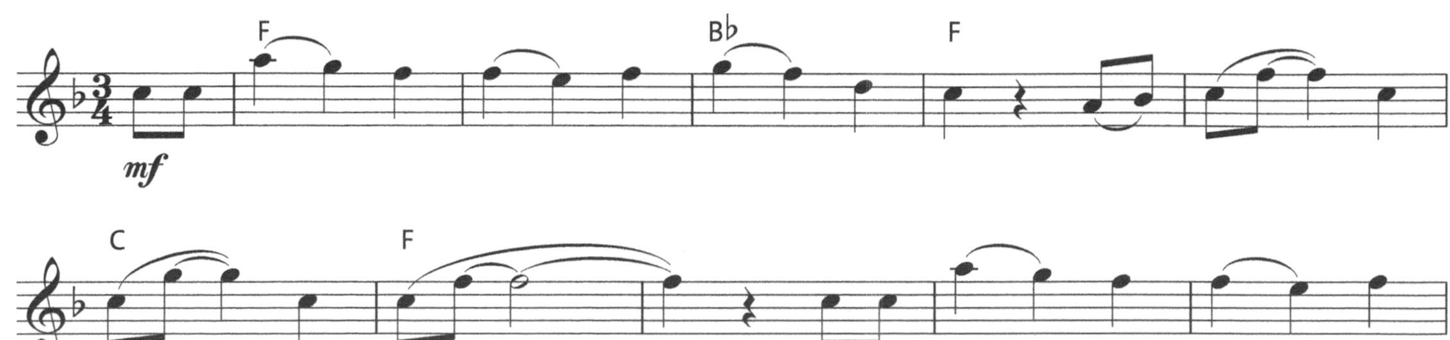

B♭ F C G7 C
Am7(♭5) D7 Gm
Am7(♭5) D7 Gm E♭ B♭/D
G7 C7 F C7 F
p
Waltz
Brahms
46
© Copyright 2006 Amsco Publications, a Division of Music Sales Corporation.
All Rights Reserved. International Copyright Secured.
Moderately
F B♭ F Dm F Dm F
mp
1. 2.
Am E7 Am Am C7 F F7
mf
B♭ G7 C7 F B♭
mp
F Dm F Dm F C7 F
p

Men Of Harlech

Welsh Traditional

Rock-A-My Soul

Spiritual

Moderate swing

Estampie

Medieval Dance

49

50 We'll Meet Again

Parker & Charles

Moderate swing

Diamonds Are A Girl's Best Friend

Styne & Robin

Lively

G

f

B♭dim7 Am7 D7

Am Am(maj7) Am7 D7

A7 Am7 D13

G7 C

mf

G Em A7 D7

G F7 E9

f

Am D13 G

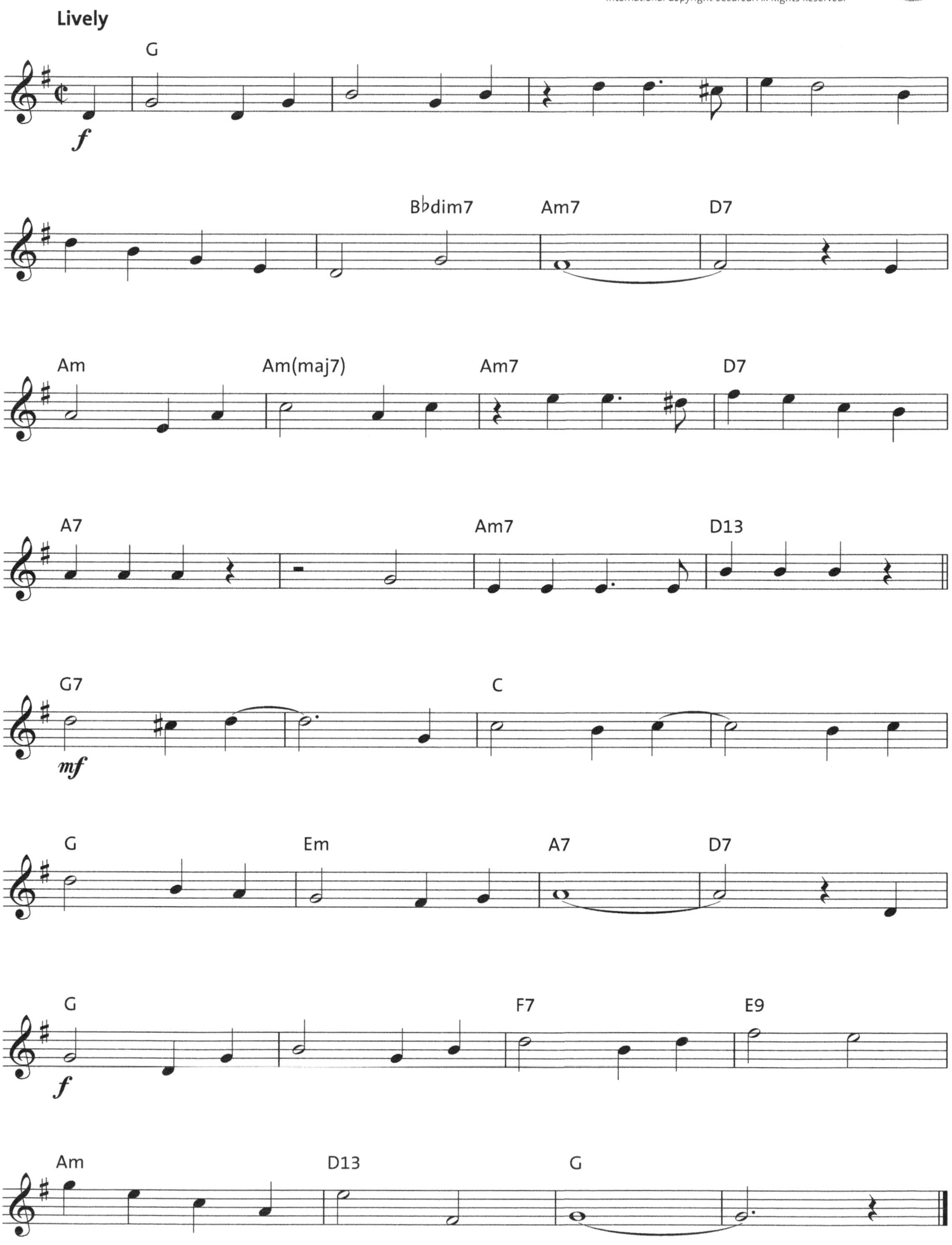

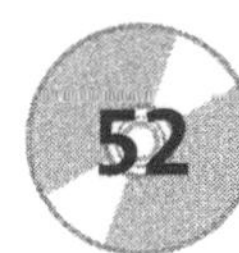

52 *Jeanie With The Light Brown Hair*

Foster

C7 F C13 F Dm F/C Gm C7
mf
F C13 F G7 C Dm/F Gsus G7 C
mp
C7/B♭ F/A B♭ F/A G7 C7
mf
f
F C13 Dm F/A B♭ Csus C7 F
mf
p

53 *Emperor Quartet* (excerpt)

Beethoven

Adagio
G D G D G C G/B D G
mp
Am/C A/C♯ D G D G D G
C G/B D G Am/C A/C♯ D D7 G D7 G D7
mf

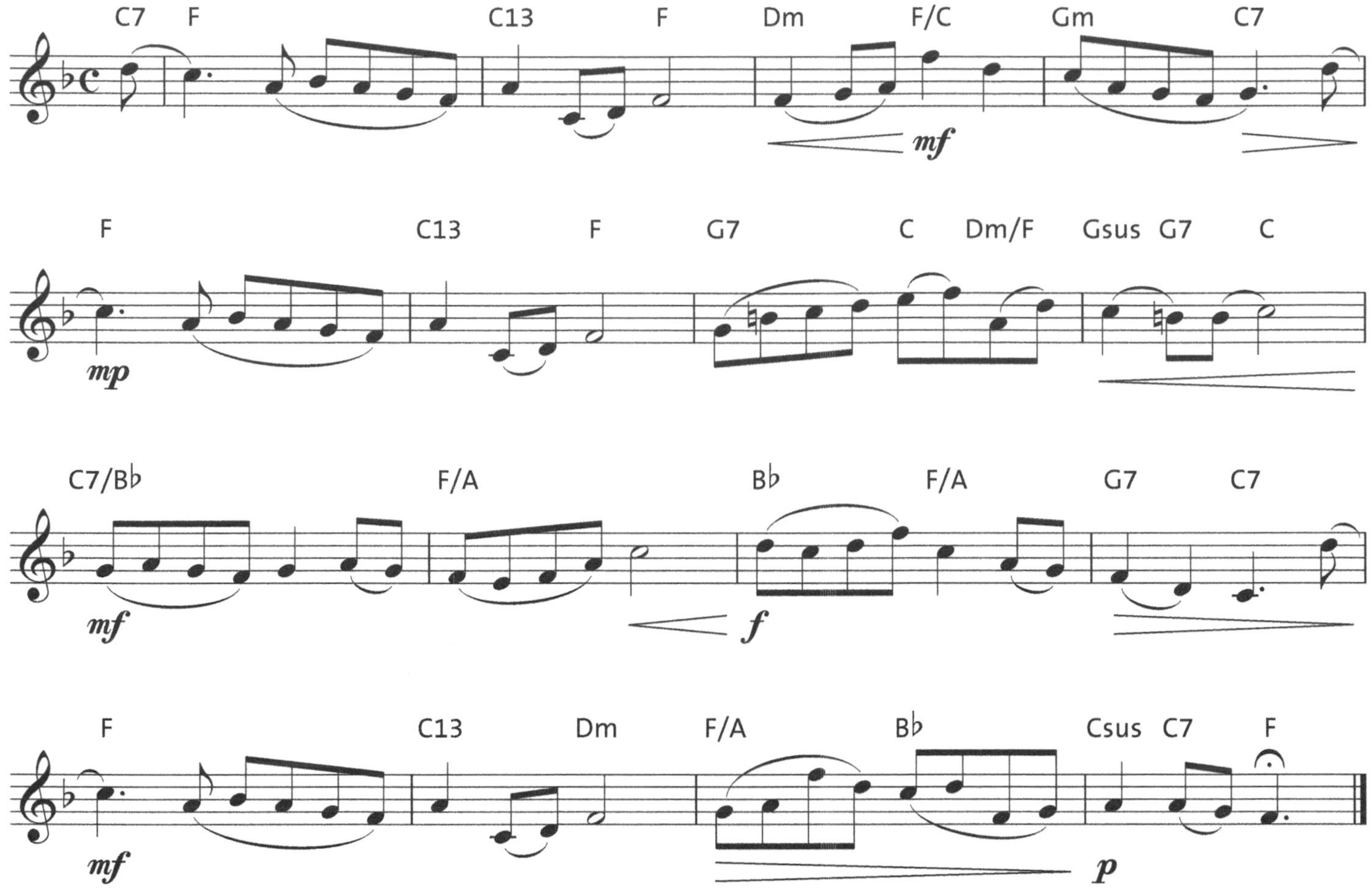

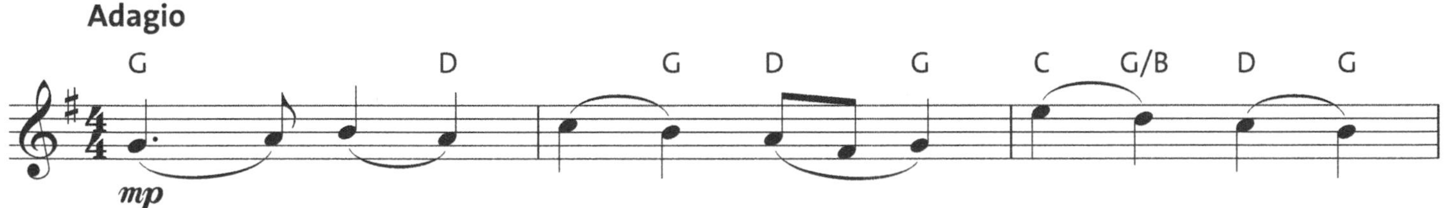

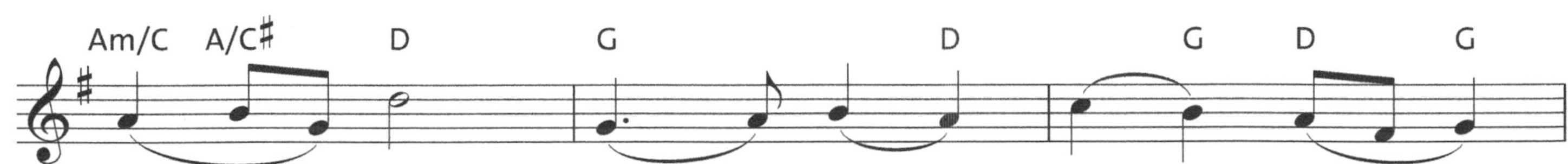

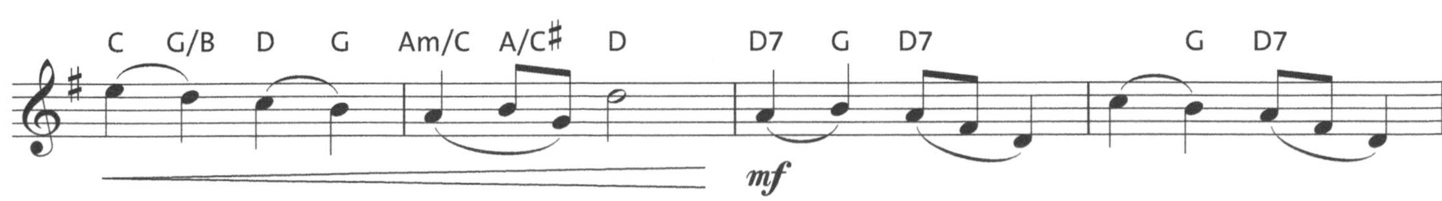

G Em A7 D7 G C G
f
C G/B D7/A G Am/C G C G/D D7 G
Swan Lake (excerpt)
Tchaikovsky
54
© Copyright 2006 Amsco Publications, a Division of Music Sales Corporation.
All Rights Reserved. International Copyright Secured.
Andante cantabile
Dm Gm Dm Gm Dm Gm
mf
Dm Gm Dm Gm Dm
mp
C7 Am Gm E7 A Dm
mf
C7 Am Gm E♭
mp
E7 A7 Dm Gm Dm B♭m
f
Dm Gm Dm B♭m A7 Dm
p

Polovtsian Dance

Borodin

Andante moderato

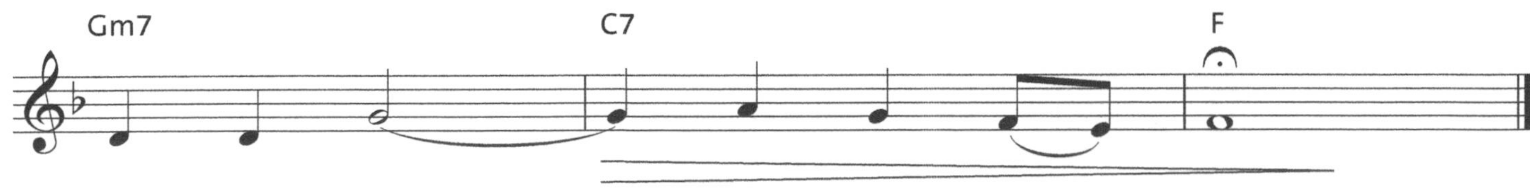

Dark Eyes

Russian Traditional

56

Jupiter (from *The Planets Suite*)

Holst

Andante

D G A7 D F♯m G A Bm A

mf

G A7 D G A D A Bm

mp

A D A D G Em Bm A G D

G Em Bm A G A D F♯m G A

mf

Bm A G A D G A D

A Bm A D A D G Em Bm A G

D G Em Bm A G A D F♯m

f

G A Bm A G A D G A D

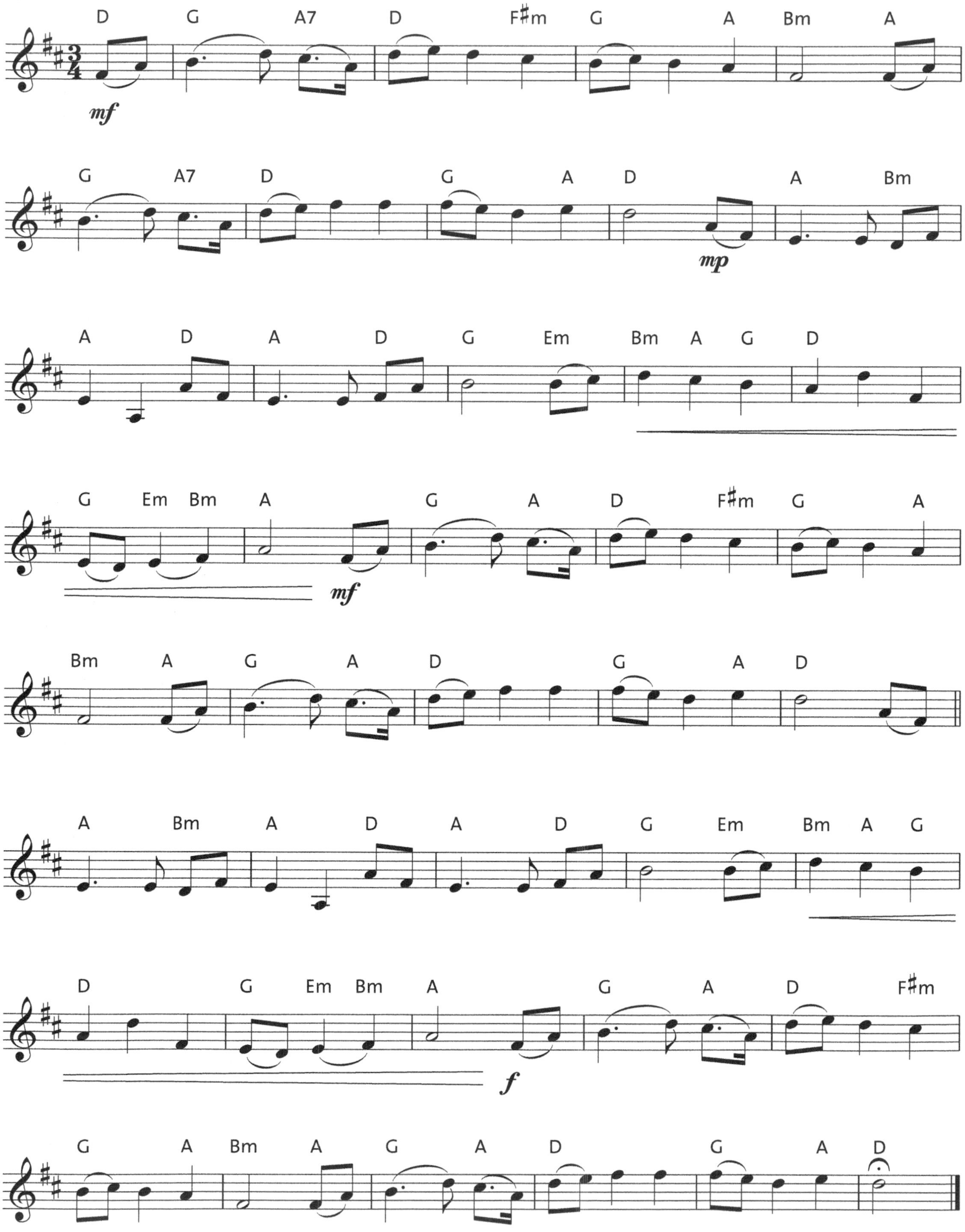

Bring Me Sunshine

Kent & Dee

58

The Frim Fram Sauce

Ricardel & Evans

Moderate swing

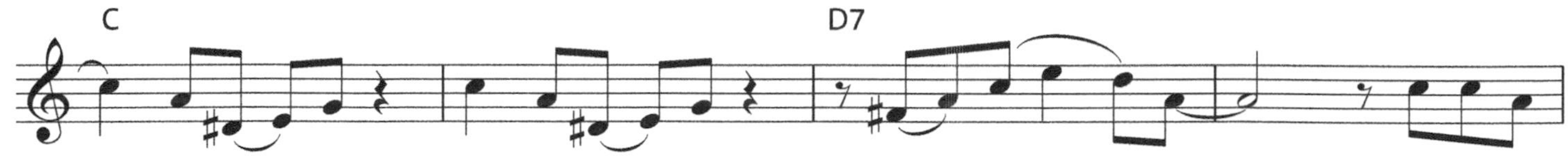

Try A Little Tenderness

Woods, Campbell & Connelly

60

Grand March (from *Aida*)

Verdi

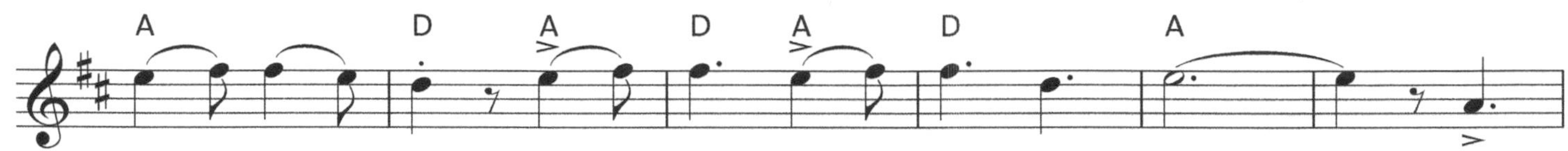

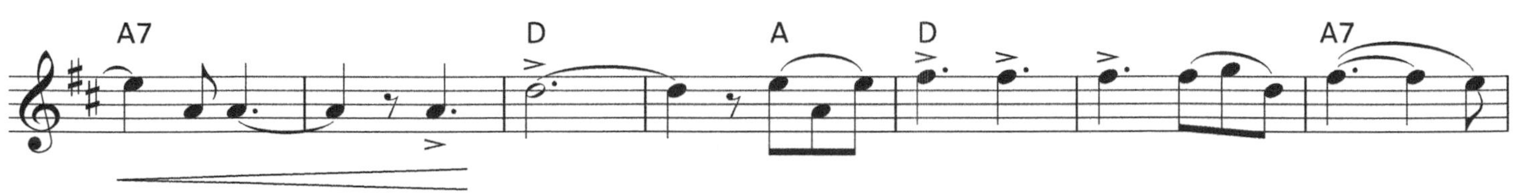

Radetsky March

Strauss

Moderato

E♭

B♭7 *sim.* E♭ B♭ F7 B♭ B♭7

E♭

F7 B♭7 E♭ A♭ B♭7 E♭ ***Fine***

A♭ *sim.* E♭

B♭7 A♭ E♭ B♭7 E♭

B♭7 E♭ G7 Cm G7 Cm

G Cm G Cm G Cm G Cm G ***D.S. al Fine***

Nellie The Elephant

Hart & Butler

A7 D A7 D
G D A7 D
p
E7 A E7 A7
D G D
f
A7 D E7 A7
D G D
A7 D Em7 A7
D

John Brown's Body

American Traditional

Medium swing

In The Hall Of The Mountain King (from *Peer Gynt*)

Grieg

65

Fig Leaf Rag

Joplin

66

CD backing tracks

1 Tuning Notes
2 Camptown Races
3 Early One Morning
4 Santa Lucia
5 Poor Little Buttercup
6 My Bonnie Lies Over The Ocean
7 Romance No. 1
8 Kalinka
9 Coventry Carol
10 Molly Malone
11 Banana Boat Song
12 Telstar
13 Satin Doll
14 Coasts Of High Barbary
15 Babu Sau
16 Mama Don't Allow
17 La Cucaracha
18 Shenandoah
19 Turkey In The Straw
20 Steal Away
21 Over The Hills
22 Catch A Falling Star
23 Underneath The Arches
24 Ding Dong Merrily On High
25 By The Rivers Of Babylon
26 Old Folks At Home
27 Bach Minuet
28 Jurassic Park Theme
29 Angel Eyes
30 Dick's Maggot
31 Nobody Knows
32 British Grenadiers
33 Mozart Minuet
34 Greensleeves
35 The Hebrides Overture
36 The Keel Row
37 Mexican Hat Dance
38 Perdido
39 Blackadder Theme
40 Deep River
41 Das Wandern
42 Hatikvah
43 The Ash Grove
44 Bill Bailey
45 Tit Willow
46 Brahms Waltz
47 Men Of Harlech
48 Rock-A-My Soul
49 Estampie
50 We'll Meet Again
51 Diamonds Are A Girl's Best Friend
52 Jeanie With The Light Brown Hair
53 Emperor Quartet
54 Swan Lake
55 Polovtsian Dance
56 Dark Eyes
57 Jupiter
58 Bring Me Sunshine
59 The Frim Fram Sauce
60 Try A Little Tenderness
61 Grand March
62 Radetsky March
63 Nellie The Elephant
64 John Brown's Body
65 In The Hall Of The Mountain King
66 Fig Leaf Rag

How to use the CD

The tuning notes on track 1 are A, D, G, and E, respectively.

After track 1, the backing tracks are listed in the order in which they appear in the book. Look for the symbol in the book for the relevant backing track.

Listen for the clicks at the start of each track: depending on the tempo and time signature, each track will have clicks for one or two bars before the melody begins. When the melody starts with an anacrusis, the click will also play for the first part of the bar.